THE OTHER HAND

Also by Dabney Stuart
The Diving Bell
A Particular Place

The
Other Hand

Poems by DABNEY STUART

LOUISIANA STATE UNIVERSITY PRESS

BATON ROUGE

1974

6/197
am. Li

ISBN 0–8071–0076–5
Library of Congress Catalog Card Number 73–91775
Copyright © 1974 by Dabney Stuart
Manufactured in the United States of America

Designed by Albert Crochet. Composed in 10/12 point
Electra by Typoservice Corporation, Indianapolis,
Indiana. Printed and bound by Thomson-Shore,
Dexter, Michigan.

A number of the poems published here first appeared in
the following periodicals: Antaeus, Back Door, Chicago
Tribune Magazine, Crazy Horse, Greenfield Review,
Humanist, Inlet, Jam To-Day, Lillabulero, Mediter-
ranean Review, Mill Mountain Review, Mo' Juice,
Monmouth Review, North American Review, Ohio
Review, Paintbrush, Phoenix, Place, Poetry Miscellany,
Poetry Northwest, Prairie Schooner, Quarterly Review
of Literature, Quartet, Shenandoah, Southern Poetry
Review: A Decade of Poems, Southern Review, and
Tri-Quarterly.

"Idyll," "The Trial," "Tourist," and Part 1 of "Nomad"
originally appeared in the New Yorker.
"Arrival" originally appeared in the New American Review.
"The Broken City" was the Phi Beta Kappa ceremonial
poem at The College of William and Mary in 1967.

This is Mike's book

Ja, das Entsetzliche lächelte . . . Selten
hast du so zärtlich gelächlet, Mutter. Wie sollte
er es nicht lieben, da es ihm lächelte.

—Rilke, *The Third Elegy*

Anyone who cannot come to terms with his life while
he is alive needs one hand to ward off a little his
despair over his fate—he has little success in this—
but with his other hand he can note down what he
sees among the ruins.

—Kafka, *Diaries*

Contents

Poems about Poetry

The Real World

The Broken City

Preparations

Among the Bric-a-Brac of Apology
He found nothing
Fit for his purpose
And left on a shelf under the counter
The map of its language

He closed the doors of Theories Ltd
Himself   for good
Preferring to serve other terms

The avenue widened

In the Basement of Used Names
He asked for his own
And was given the alphabet

In the Shop of Strangers
He chose the statuette of a tribesman
Black   bowed:
The calligraphy of rivers

Light spilled
Over the diminished buildings

At Tours of the Ruins
He made a deposit
Against a contingency his eyes mirrored
Carried a stone adz
And the shard of a lost urn
His city
With him to the Bone Wharf

Where all ships come in

The Colonist

for Bert Phillips

Behind me
The city of empty cables
Sags into itself

I remember
The echo of coins rusting
The slow dust turning the neon
To one color
The shallow streets

Everything went on
As usual
I found no trace of decisions
Could hear no lament
In the wind's corners

I said to my fear   *Precious*
And we left that place as brothers
Casting one shadow

That is all we have
To carry across the river of first chances

Will the stones surface?

Is the light waiting?

Will they give us a name?

Nostalgia

Theme: the child's eye
As the foundation of a city

Scene: quay
With dancers
At one of the twilights

The music of sails

Tableau: woman
With urn
Bearing a relief of the sea's edge
As a totem

I would liken this
To the shard in your basement
Your daughter's delicacy with pins
The color of Cheer

The pieces dissemble
Their sources

And there is little to hope for
Now
When the skull under this trifling skin
Is no more luminous
Than a stone

Pied Piper

All the alleys began turning
To themselves
My shadow started
Hugging the cracked glass of basement windows
I saw rats moving in it

Where is your forage? I called to them
And they nestled against my voice

We followed that music through the city
I could not tell you the crowds
Which praised us
Nor the unison of their approval

I remember them with their placards
And the windows open   our breath
Staled
We carried it with us like a chorus
Through suburbs where the antennae bowed

I thought *I have done what they want*

I do not understand them now
Coming this far with their vacuums
And pennants   into the toneless sand
                and the flat wind

                song of our remnant

Drawing garbage from a dry well

Idyll

I wait for you
In the decayed city
A silverfish in the crazed plaster

There is no place besides this left
For you
Snipped lily
Sediment of a lost vintage
Suburbanite from so far out
The ruins at the center
Seem to glitter like a gem in sunlight

When you arrive here
I will make a fine noise
Appearing

You will think it is the city
Whispering *Belovéd*

And by the friction of my quick trip
Across the down of your arm

You will know where you are

Copy

There were not enough parking places
Those who arrived late
Were sent back to the freeways

I do not remember
Who said
Nothing will come of this

But I saw men
Wearing their faces like shields

An empty sleeve
Signaling

When the microphones failed
I could hear the tearing of tickets

As a breathing

You have the speeches on file
From the last time

Print with them
This stub
Of our sore profusion

Mystic

I have seen God   O Yes
Do not fondle me with your doubt
Or your lower case vanity
Or your drugs those footnotes
To excess
I have ascended a moment
Dry as Assisi
And seen the sky turn inside out

The reflection of cities shimmered
In the same violence
Money answered the same wounds
Digestion reversed
And tasted the same

But the roots of the dead cried out
We are your children
We grow
Listen
And the alphabet flew into the sun
Taking our names with it

Leaving us
Everywhere with these losses
This incomparable
Nothing

It settles on my shoulder
Like a bird

The Ghosts

They returned
Wearing their tears   their jewels
Asking me *What have you shed?*

Skins I told them
By what other trail
Could you have followed me
This far?

It is the same face
To our eyes   they answered
See   You have no disguises

I could have borne that
As drily as I had borne
Those deaths   their sharp wreaths
The lowering transit

Had they not
Clouded my mirrors
With their breath

Teaching me
Salt

A new language

The Whore's Dream

I live in a dark convergence
Of highways
Numberless
My men
Enter me crying *Mother*

I cannot see myself

I take the moon for money
Placing it on the darkness
Like a cover on a manhole

A city rises
From the sound of that fitting
The air parting for its spires

I ride its harbor
Birds nest in my torch

Those who sleep at my feet
Complain of the cold
*What do you expect
From stone?* I ask them
Declining westward
To my other shore

When I wake
There is a black hole in the sky
Calling *Touch me   Touch me*

It is my voice

I cannot see myself

The Trial

I thought it was over

The reporters began
Leaking out of the courtroom
Bars crept up the windows
The tanks in the street shriveled

I began to breathe
The echo of doors
Locking   my judgment

It was a relief

I anticipated the mornings
Their cold dust
The stone growing in my head
All my life I thought
Will be the same day wound
Into itself   the same night

I thought it was over

But when I turned
Robes glittered above me
I rose into them
Taking my soft place
Among the judges

Sulla Writing His Memoirs

The light of my retirement flickers
But I give it no more quarter
Than I gave the rest of my enemies

No one will miss
The perfect city I never made
Not a fray in the weave
Endless

The names of the past forget themselves

Not even death my lance
Makes any difference

I have always pointed it at myself

The rest of my enemies
Found me implacable

Any way it is shed
Blood is easy

My hands
I can write nothing
You don't already know

I answer to the same sound
David's stone made in his sling

The distances of war
March toward me from every direction
Revealing their size

I fit

Rome is no bigger than my pen
See
I put it down

Mop-up Patrol

The way the sun flakes
Stone
            The sudden dust
It is hard to tell
Blanched calf shins
From the slough of lepers

These blasted eyes

We have seen
Char   diet
Of small thousands

Their bones
Shine on the black hills

We have heard
The echo of families
Burning
In the sky's mouth

There is only one weather
It is all in my mind
Circling

Each day above us
Motherwit buzzards
Who
Have their hearts in the right place
Look out for themselves

Simple

We
Second their motion

Draft Exile in Canada

The prints from the book club swelled
Cracking their frames
Fear ran in the walls
Like mice
All the words of the household stumbled

Monks on the tube shed
The only light   orient
I could hear history groping
Like a blind man in a strange room

Feature by feature
My father swept his face under the rug

Contracts

Dusty tongues moored in a dry basin

The air is clearer now
There is less to evade
I left my masks
In that country south of here

But what will I do
When there are no more borders
Pull the fire up to my chin?

Tell me mother
Governor
When war shuffles all our fingers
To one color
And the world is safe
Who will gather the ashes?

Morning After a Storm

I wake with my hand under the pillow
Like a secret

The light has resumed its borders
What is left of thunder is silent
As a fist opening

Haze stretches over the sky
Like gauze

What wound does it hide, Fancy?
What name do you have today
For your lies?

How will you figure
What remains after violence?

Have you heard
That another king said
*Wars do not necessarily mean
The ruin of the regions in which they rage?*

Between which zeroes will you put the decimal?

What will you do with the bones?

I bring you the secret of my hand
Moving toward noon

At Jamestown Island

for David Jeddie Smith

How far
Beneath the dispersed ashes
Does the quirk move
That moves these waves?

At what depth
Beneath the deranged clocks
Does the channel take its options
Veering the wide shelves?

A stale chime sounds

The remote stones

We should have settled these quarrels

There was enough time
Before our closets were air-conditioned
The switchboards perfected

See
The tern still rides
The trough's plumb and the crest's distinction
Like a buoy

Marking
Its cordial balance

Williamsburg Revisited

As in even the smallest town
Nowadays
The telephone book thickens

A carriage wheel

Six channels in every home
Deepen the illusion of choice

Colonial livery

The peacocks
Marking the palace garden
Remain serious about themselves

An aegis
Above the cobbles

Prosper

While the same deliberate road
Runs between the James' margin and the marsh
Shunning the toy ships

For the island

Where it circles a thin chance
Settling
Which the Pacific turned back
To us, to this restoration

The Broken City

The walls have crumbled
As though into new buildings

Citizens
I had told them
When they walked
Door to door
In their stories of fear
Citizens
No bomb will raze this city

It will come I said
Because stone seeks its own level

I said *The shape of your hands*
Is responsible
Every city
Comes to resemble
The fingerprints of its builders

Look at your hands
I told them
You need no other mirror
Of the future

But it was worse
Than talking to stone
They fell away from me

Echoes of their voices
Said "Stay then
We have nothing to do with this"

I watched them leave
Thinking
You will scrape the same sky
Again
Roofing your supplication

I looked at my hands
Thinking

The thickest fingers
May touch in the hum of ruin
The beginning of song

Thinking *If you wait*
You will hear
What you promised yourselves
Once
Among these foundations

I watched them leave
Forgetting themselves

It is not that I am
Alone
The mortar ticks loose from crevices
A thin wind dusts the rubble

I have found
Initials imbedded in unlikely places
And a bird's nest in a rotting mortise

Everything is exposed

The evening and
The morning
Accomplish the same sound

I move
In a space without doorways
Always at an open window

Saying to no one
In particular
This is our city now
The stones have arrived
At their true places
Everything fits

It is possible at last
To live here

Nomad

Tourist

He chose the Mediterranean
Because it was the cradle of something

He did not expect so many islands
The flat faces
Such stranded passion

Old waters shrugged him off
The light sieved him
He heard no sirens
But at evening expectation hung in the air
Like musk

He began to understand
This was no voyage he could return from

And sits
The miles done
In his apartment   his door
Unlocked

Waiting to come home

The Other Sky

When rain hung in the mountains
The other sky wavered

Wind currying the light

The grass fraying
Fields approaching their edges
The river shifting its stones

In time

I should have charted that motion
But the season lifted
Like a weather

The skies merged
A flat storm settling

Since then I have staggered my absences
Coming back by a late map
Reading a tame shadow
A constant ceiling

The corrected roads

New Year's

I have walked this whole road
How many times
Past imagining
And never surrendered

No one was ever armed
But I have my own thorns

It is not as though there were beasts
Either
But I keep my threats ready
Like a net

I asked the mirrors
For directions

They all point the same way

When was it I turned to you
And heard the ditches sing
Farther?

I took it for a promise

But you see
How accurately the footprints wait
How carefully they weather

Remaining

Deer

Animal Forest Park, New Hampshire

Their hesitant circling
Their precarious ribs
Their voices
          balked

I offered them my hands
It's all I have I said
They continued their hunger

Tell me your questions I said
I will teach you to climb them
The sky lowered

They lay down by a gate
Their necks turned in the dust like keys
Nothing
Opened

What else can I do?
I asked no one myself

I covered their eyes with pennies
But it did not protect me
They said nothing as usual
They looked
The fences in their eyes grew

                                        I

Left them
Thinking *Everything*
Diminishes
Except loss

Their eyes will break with it
Spilling through the barred distance
To you and me their

Keepers

Pardon

I do not find
Your hand easily

I have flailed through the months
Their cobwebs
The years   the cellars

I would wake
To find the rats nuzzling my throat
Were my own hands

I spent a season
Giving the walls their names
They absorbed them
                    I do not believe
Stones sing
But I have heard my shadow laughing
Among them

When the echoes subsided
I climbed on my shoulders
I could see through the bars of ice

Two children pitched pennies
For my eyes   The hands
Of the town clock pointed at me
The streets began to turn my way

I confess I cried I'm coming out

I do not find your hand
Easily   the years   the doorways

Rebound

How long did it last, six weeks?
Hardly enough time to burnish brass

And weren't you the girl
I dreamed of midnight   midwinter?
Wasn't it your window
In the shifty tenements of sleep
I fastened against like frost?

Tell me didn't I tell you
How many times the way it was
Rubbing that lantern like an old jinx
Believing nothing   my genie
Until you came?

Have you no heart for legend?

But nothing breaks unless
It is the pauper's vision of himself
Next time I shall take the streets
Proud of this illusion
I hold out like a tin cup

Pregnancy

Six months ago six
Little months she left
The dew to itself

Mornings

The sun rising alone
Over the flat chances of the world

Explorers daring at noon
The four corners of her window

Now   lying beside herself
She wakes
Slowly to the mapless panes

A moist shadow

The tilted field

Travel Poster

How many others
Were spurred to tell her
They were not the shadows of absence
Nor the echoes of Goodyear
Across her tooled garden?

Myself
I added
Even at the instant your eyes crumble
In our riding
You yield only a small place
Where I leave nothing
Alive

Has anyone ever
Been here?

I drove off her map
On which all highways turned
Back to town   back
To her stable

Where the literal horse
Bore her astride every distance

Her thighs
Quivering the world home

La Belle

First light finds
You
Tossed among sleeves rumpled
Leftovers   You close
The blinds

What else have you reached for

Shadows fret your thighs
We have managed no such
Music
In spite of the practice
Play
Kindling on the taut sheets

What of those long beds
Woman
Have you eaten my ashes

Out of doors
The sun spills down the awnings
The early world swims in it
Waking

You keep
To bed   fingering
Your sachet of dried seeds

Vision

Three years after the fire died
I huddled in the fireplace

The ashes freezing
The flue leaking my share of the odor
Of billboards

All the highways led here
Following me

I thought the room
Empty
And saw you
Leaning against the abrupt mantle

Miles off

Your face stale with longing
Staring through me into the stones

Air for a Lost Lady

I will make an homage
To your wide pores   coins
For my lust

To the diplomacy of your small mouth
Wary of its entreaties   preferring
My coarse tongue
To the border of promises

To your breasts
For which my lips formed no enclosure
Save themselves

To the broad tendencies of your
Sex
By which I was uprooted a thousand
Fold

And to the dissolution therein

But most of all
In this language of distances
I regret
The tips of your blank womb

Advice to the Lovelorn

I will try not to
Speak of death
Offering his claw as a gift
No

But of that other dissimulation

You remember its voices
The thread crackling in the gravestone
The coal under the ash
Humming   Bird
In your throat and its song
Flown to some other season
Beckoning

Of course

Tendresse
And the ticking of sonnets

But you bed in a different
Hour
The mice run up the clock
The dust folds its hands on the mirror

Where the crab moves
There is only one month

And its name rhymes with nothing

Gaps

Friends
We have uses for each other
Ignitions
The world turns

We cross

It is silly
To get worked up over these
Graphs our lives
Paychecks

Oh
You have your dreams do you?
Burning?

Into which one do you dream
Of being born?

My useless places celebrate themselves
Water moving over its stones
To no end

            The space between light
And its cinder
Widening

In the room made for him
My son
Sleeps with one eye open

The Refugee

While he talked the wireless man listened
For news of the fog lifting
The storm cutting down the mountains.

He'd thought it was midnight when he started
But who knew what time it was
The weather all over you like this.

He'd lost his clothes on the barbed wire
Piece by piece   *It was all right*
He said   *The fog fit all right.*

He thought he'd cut himself once
But couldn't see what it was
He wiped off his thigh   *Damn fog*

Felt like blood anyhow   Half the time
He had a hard on he said
The way that stuff seemed to love him.

The rest of us sat there thinking we saw him
A woman knitted a sweater with one arm
I looked for a window.

He'd kept the right direction
Eating everything in sight
When he ate his eyes he began to have visions.

He said he saw men armed with fences
Barbed wire fences bordering a road
His limbs flapped like clothing on the barbs.

He walked down the middle
He saw his penis standing ahead of him like a lighthouse
His eyes blinked from it like a beacon.

Steered clear of that he said
*The worst was thinking I'd been walking
In the same place   That was the worst.*

He said the fog kept him from being sure
He said he just kept going   Kept going
He said we didn't know how relieved he was to be here.

The fog caressed me   My groin ached
His voice burned my eyes   *We couldn't bear*
Your beating the door I said

We had to let you out.

The Detractors

Cheerless
They sit in the bleachers their
Eyes

Pennants score the horizon

I have seen them as one
Body
Rise
Clotting the east with a black light

They bow
Fingering their stubs   thinking
We never lose
                         Their language
Equals the square root of
No   deathless
As glass
They follow it into tomorrow their
Mirror   giving

Them to themselves

The Elect

They ascend into themselves
Above the figures of shame
As a crow flees its shadow

They angle toward noon
Were the sun a needle
They would thread it with their steep pride
And sew *God* on the sky their
Sampler

But all light
Waking
Shales from them

If they could look down
They would see
The ground starred with it

If they could return
They would congregate in the cedars
Of the North   their locked eyes
The color of snow

Reflecting
The bright hearths of the lost

St. David's Church

Radnor, Pennsylvania

It retains
A capacity for shadows

The stained wood carries
A long odor of prayer

The walls are thick with it
Breathing

It dances with the shadows

If this air
A distillation of voices
Is the echo
Of *Sanctuary*
It is the same sound
Anchored
In the black streets

A ceiling of refuge

As specific as maples
Soughing
                    their shadows
Dancing
Across   the stones of this place

Nomad

1. THE FUTURE

There is no trace I
Have mislaid the usual footprints
Dog-eared pages love
Letters even the alphabet moves
By a lost map   Someone
Must have come here to say this   What

As though something
Salt
Had stopped following
Me

Once I remember
I said *The light in the walls
Is dying*
But what did that mean

Nothing
A sort of music

And I remember
The cracks in their faces my eyes
Forget
The shapes of disgust

It had something to do
With the dust of cities
Settling   Was there
Water

Well I have given
Mirages to those who asked
Passing   They never came back
Perhaps
They were real

But I can tell there is only one
Direction
And the stones with their past
Lead everywhere

41

2. Memory

I said *Everywhere*
But today they drift Northward
A ritual tendency

Where is this desert   I have
Felt it before   in my bones
But where are the coordinates
For that   Are there voyages
Within voyages

It settles
Nowhere
Containing my arrivals
                                        cups
They run over
Their greetings are absorbed
Into the stones

Surely my name
Shall disappear into its origins
Ice
Or something which keeps no weather
Always wishing
To be spoken

3. Death

It will rise in the east
Fluent
And exhaust the desert with light
An oasis
Slaking all exclamation

The echoes of thirst will subside
I will empty the glass of my deceptions
On the stones my tongue's
Haven

Those who have listened
Will hear them sing more lucidly
Than the emperor's nightingale

Who knew
To what dry brilliance
All mirages converge

Major Work

When I died
The light around me   that
Mold
Cracked
Fell away

Such dust arose
As would accompany
The breaking of vows

It ascended so finely
Shattered
It seems whole

A sky
Under which I begin

Again

Poems about Poetry

Poetry: A Lecture on the Discrete

Why these masks

These rescues of the will in the will's tangents

These cages of possibility considering music

These dark
Prizes competing   These masks
Portioning light

It is not a matter of fashion
Wear this wear that
No
Nor the fizz of reputation
In some blank eye

But an entertainment
Of what might otherwise be lost

Waking

Singular fictions through which to embark

Toward a face

The Animals

One of them is silence
Its hide is seek
Cornered in the valley of its calling
It echoes
Like absence

Another is longing
It drinks
From the pool of its own reflection
All day its weight dreams

                              darkness
A third   whose shape
Skins my fingers
                    Heel I say
Heel
Following

            They bring me their meadow
            Offering its seasons of hunger
            We fatten

            A peaceable kingdom

Aesthetics

1

Once upon a time
There was only one face
Seeking itself

Kiss me it said
To the prince   that impossible
Poem
And began
Deciding among echoes
Paring the ample music

2

Then something a bone
Grinned
Focusing the darkness
Crows began gathering in the cedars
Snow fell in my side

I placed my hand on that knowledge
Weathering

3

Now in a space of mirrors
There is only the one voice
Dancing

Absorbing
The refractions of silence

The Demons

1. ABSENCE

A poet has written *Mysteries*
Will come to those who need them

Not intending to shame me
But I am shamed

Since I must conclude I do not
Need them

He has also written *The blind*
In Spring stuff their eyes with leaves
Compounding their blindness

Now in October
I rake my eyes

2. DISPOSITION

Seasonless themselves
They sense our seasons

If we ease into the stems of Spring
Grow lush
With our own promise

They recede
To the rim of our vacation

They do not extend us the comfort
Of their contempt
Knowing their distance

Serves.
Only the rake's scratch

And the crackle of the leaf
Burning
The dry flare of our ruse

Consuming
Itself   leaving

A cold necessity
From which we can grow nothing
Will summon them again alert

Them
To our return

3. In a Domestic Place

The space
Between the fire in the hearth
And the firelight in the eye
Their space

The time
Coincident with the son's cry
In the night and his father's dream
Of waking
Their time

Their rhythm
All singing
Shadows

4. Prayer

Enter my eyes
When they are cold enough

Weather me
Beyond seasons

Contend me

Contend

The Real World

Arrival

What do you love
A voice said
Myself

Where does that get you

These are the wrong questions

My daughter has begun
To linger with pages
To sleep under her pillow
Collect flies   She has told
Me
The snow is black under the mountains

She lives elsewhere
My son
Addresses the light as though he would dance
With it
He requests messages
His eyes
Read me in no language I understand
They are his
Partner

Often when the evening
Forgets its hour and the day turns
Into itself my wife
Remembers
The years before me
She keeps her
Distances

I would have it no other way

These are the wrong answers

They are not answers

Where does that get you

Here

Wake

In the room of the dead   his
Room
The immaculate sheets
Wait   deserted

A feast, the consummation
Of a marriage?
           I carry
The question across the hall
To the room where the sun sets
Its light meeting a light
In the mahogany it burnishes
The crust of his eyes
Follows me   burning

What is this coming together?

In the hall someone
With a picnic basket
Sends me for mourning
I carry her voice a lantern
Into the closet
             The lush
Gowns billow   splendid
Rank with caprice

I end here   the echo
        of departure

Who is dancing?

Where has he gone?

A Minor Elegy

He took volcanoes lightly
And the naming of love
But considered waking
A time for caution
And gave his life to it

The latches on all his doors were soundless
When there was no way out
He rearranged them
Being much given
To the dignity of approaches

He wanted no more
Than to teach his shadow its place
Passing over the split pavement
Balancing

The decorum of leaves

The guests at his funeral
Found the coffin dusted with pumice

A forgotten air

And they kept his word for themselves

The Heir

Father
I have taken my language   a tent
With me into the desert

It does not keep
The wind your will
From me
            the wind

The sand your voice
Becomes its floor
Wherever I pitch it
            the sand

Your voice the finest stones
Wind-driven says
Come whenever you can

I answer   *Here*

And the mirages
Toward which I move
From which I move
Recede into themselves

Taxing all distances

Table Talk

In the thick of dessert
I said to myself
Son   There was

A long pause   I
Heard a diamond burning

When the coffee came
I said to myself
Father   The silence

Condensed   I saw it
Rain dust

Raising my empty glass
I said *Friends*

Toasting the world

Losses

They thrive in a cold air
Their own season
Changeless

He has no other communion

Their darkness breaks his eyes   those wide
Occasions
            No
Crazed light under the sun
Rivals that sharp brilliance
Abiding its own calendar
Timing his grief

What peace have they made
His far daughter with her one
Raw decade   crackling

Whoever of his women took him
For more than he was   surrendering
Their need to the bright promises
The years without edges

Or his words   bent
To their fire   listening

Do they hear his voice   still
Entering the storms

Ascending

And the rod his hand
Raised
To the lightning

Making Love

The times I have turned this key
Asking *Who's there?*
Entering the echo

Mobs of desire
Throning my name
Her clothes floating my fingers

I planted myself in the great rooms
Dispersing those voices

I served
           denying
No hazard
Neither the loud nipple
Nor the shrewd thigh
Nor the place itself
Mothering

Was it to come here
I scrapped the billboards?
Tunneled beneath textbooks?
Was it to lose my head
This way
I starved my clichés?
Is this no different
From that other boneyard?

What grows   What grows
On the way to itself?

Who's there?
Does any man fit
These spaces
Opening

The orient darkness

Keeping the flesh going

Make-up

It's your only face
—Savon Clair ad

I never expected you
To throw out your brushes

To let the powdery slab   a cheek
Fall
The lashes of one eye
Remain on the dresser
Like a dead centipede
A lid drip off
Your lips stay in the tube

I begin to see
Your only face
Love

It is like looking through a mirror

I will be
Faithful to this

Other Women Cloy

Woman
Why do you bring me
This wary cheek?

Though you have turned the other
A thousand ways
It is always the same

No matter how many angles
Your eyes try
They make the same corner

                   where you
Find me
No king consorting with sonnets
But a flagrant boy
Needing your petulant wishbone

You keep
Bringing it back
Unbroken

Nothing comes true

You are as devious as a billboard

But I play   I buy
Wondering
What we can do
With your wide reserve

Bible Story

to my wife

This will astonish you
But it begins
With the texture of your flesh
Warming toward love

Oh I have always believed
Desire has its rainbows
When I was younger
They bore more traffic than the Bay Bridge

They have brought me
To the light on your neck something like
Gold

Begins

My energy focusing
You   It is
All beginning

When I was younger
I had my targets
The devious temples   insurance
Men coddling their premiums
The national league
And what not

You know

The separate world
Looming above David

Now my own life is Goliath
Twitching under the cuffs you launder

If I wanted
I wouldn't know where
To sling the stone

Directions

Go, poem
Show her this ceremony
Continues
Deathless tell her
As she the thorns persist

But for the ease of her hand upon them
They would be bloomless
The desert my flesh monotonous
With their crackling

Tell her it would be all murder
And the cleaning of weapons
Without her gentleness
                                    As it is
No one approaches
Knighthood
Save through this chink her
Restraint

Do not remind her Loss
Disregards all but this
Song
            Instead
Say the difficulty
Of hearing the claims of survival
Piecemeal
Becomes more resonant
Because her music does not surrender
Its designs
To anything   including
Me

Vantages

I was told
Not to worry   the turnpike
Obeyed its signs
The tolls were infrequent
Visibility
Reasonable

If I sat still
I would arrive

Somewhere

Between a strict grade
And a charming straightaway
The road left its bed
Trestling

I could see all the way down
On both sides   a river

Rising

The tires began peeling
The pavement trembled
The windshield cracked under the pressure

It was all I could do
To break through the guardrail

All the way down
My slow choice
I kept thinking
That river will be adequate
To the rubble

And *There is something*
In space
I had not counted on

I left the car everywhere
It landed

Took my place on a stone
Of the wreckage

Watched a sudden covey
Thrill the span under my exit

Letting the cause of that sensible vacancy
Carry on

Derivations

Wakeful
My son frets   sounds
Dubious as these my own

              Not yet certain   reluctant
              To concur   undetermined
              Questionable, as in
              The dubious distinction of being the first
              To know

Child, love, one love
Leads to another   To your crying
I gave mine   leaves   pressed in time

              To vex   chafe   corrode
              To be troubled   to be worn
              Away   to eat and be
              Eaten
                        The ridges on the neck
              Of a stringed instrument
                                        An ornamental
              Design with numerous
              Small openings   often done
              In relief
                        The headdress
              Of a Medieval lady   interlaced

My lexicon considers all these
Sources of music   as in *We learn to play*
The frets
          or *Your mother wears*
Her fret gracefully, accustomed

It is no more than
A higher plane of regard

              The cessation of sleep
              Alertness   A vigil
              Particularly for the dead   sometimes
              Accompanied by festivity
                                        The visible
              Track of turbulence left by a ship

          Moving through water

                                        What remains
          Consequence

This too bruits a harmony   as
We love under the sun
Waking

My son   I hear you
Through the porous walls between us
I hear your brother outdoors
In his afternoon   sounding
His young friendships

The levels of our world

The interlacings we call through

I hear

In your turn
Hear me

Speak our language

The Real World

What meanest thou, O sleeper?
—Jonah 1:6

1. WAKING

When I began
To dance with my shadow
The grass softened   I felt
The ground give with my step

I heard the roots of an aspen
Probing the slow stone
Deepening
Veining the strata
I heard the sound of its leaves
Beginning there   brightening

I saw
The sun rising and the sun
Setting in the same
Twilight   The seasons
Observed each other
Bearing my names
My voice undertook their borders
Merging

Resonant with dreams   I said to you
Here   This is my ambience   When I descend
Into the pool of sleep   suspended from the line
Of myself lowering into myself   I am learning
The buried words   I am dancing among the stones
Darkening   As a fish moves deeply among stones
Where his need gathers   I am learning to speak
Here   at the roots of my waking

Waking   I said   *Here is the music*
I dance to   My shadow's music   I bring it back

2. TWO DREAMS

On the low shore, alone, inordinate
    He casts the dark line himself
Singing it arcs born by its own weight
    Down. He feels it go taut

70

In the uncertain light, the aquatic
    Something a fish in time
With his instinctive strike
    Runs for the sudden spillway, lengthening

The line that connects them he keeps tight.
    The fish leaps breaking and bearing
His water, drops out of sight.
    Holding the slack line, severed

He sees a cat rising, taking its place
    On the spillway top, strutting
Holding the stripped fish carcass in its teeth
    Its eyes burning and dry. His face.

He went down into the sides of the ship
To be broken

The sea wrought   He went
            down into it
Weeds wrapped his head

He went into the sides of the fish
Its bones enclosed him   his shadow
All darkness

A rising   the dry land
He sat in the gourd's shadow
Which the worm hollowed   listening

The ribs of the mountains
The bars of the earth   the fish

Waiting

3. THE REMORA

                        necesse est ut prius de
                        magnete sapientum te instruam

Small fish nowhere I know
Whose grip detained great Antony
At sea, and taught Caligula delay
Stilling his headlong prow

71

I have as small as you
A stone that burns nowhere I know
To draw you drawing me   dark opening
To dark and breaking day

Each other's deeper surfacing